# Be Brave not Bitter

'It was all because he Lied'

Wakiekie Reid

Wakiekie Reid

Po box 1530

Stockbridge, GA 30281

[wakiekie@reiditgroup.com](mailto:wakiekie@reiditgroup.com)

This book is dedicated to my older sisters who showed me how to be brave even when I was bruised.

To my loving kind and patient daughter Amber, who witnessed the bruises of my heart and placed a bandage on my spirit with her respect and obedience.

To my kindhearted and protective son Khian, who never stop giving me hugs on my cloudy days or judged my mistakes as a single mother and my many failed attempts to understand him becoming a man.

A special thanks to my big brother James, for showing me that a MAN will always conduct himself as a man when he has first learned the meaning from God what is expected of a man.

# Table of Contents

Introduction ..................................................................... 6

*Chapter 1* **Who Are You?** ............................................... 9

*Chapter 2* **We were not prepared** ............................... 10

*Chapter 3* **Was your Blueprint legible?** ..................... 12

*Chapter 4* **Puppy Love** ................................................. 14

*Chapter 5* **First Love First deceit** ............................... 16

*Chapter 6* **Becoming a Woman too soon** ................... 18

*Chapter 7* **A new me** ..................................................... 20

*Chapter 8* **Pain with Purpose** ...................................... 22

*Chapter 9* **He was all that I had** .................................. 24

*Chapter 10* **When We know better, we do better.** ..... 26

*Chapter 11* **Pressing Through** ..................................... 28

*Chapter 12* **When your space is shared but it is treated different** .................................................................... 30

*Chapter 13* **So What** ................................................. 32

*Chapter 14* **Saddling up when it hurts** ..................................... 34

*Chapter 15* **Sacred seclusion** ...................................... 36

*Chapter 16* **Bruised but not broken "My pain healed me "** 38

*Chapter 17* **Re introduce yourself to yourself** ...................... 40

*Chapter 18* **Moving Forward** ........................................ 42

*Chapter 19* **Let go of the old embrace the new** ..................... 44

*Chapter 20* **Be Brave not Bitter** ................................... 46

# Introduction

The man of the house, the man in sports, the man at his workplace the man to the children he raises, overall, the man. He is designed to be strong to protect to secure and cherish the heart of a woman. What happens when all of those qualities are met then the man you trust and love makes you regret the day you ever allowed him to have so much authority over your happiness, your home, your choices? So much power over. When a woman loses herself into the control of a man her heart becomes Bruised. In this dialogue you will of the brokenness of a woman's heart, how she healed and realized how to get through the deceit and misconception of what was portrayed as Love. A heart can be bruised and even broken, but when we learn how to love properly, we will not be bitter.

# WOMAN

As soon as we can understand we are told behind every good man we must stand, as a stronger woman.
Often, we are lost trying to find our purpose, the pressure to be perfect and be strong at times we
Forget who we are or who we wanted to be. It is not expected that man understands the role of a woman, the weight, the purpose of being a woman, it is okay if he doesn't but it's not okay if we don't.
Genesis 2:24 Then the LORD God made woman from the rib he had taken out of man, and he brought her to the man. 23 the man said, "this is now bone of my bones and flesh of my flesh; she shall be called "woman, for she was taken out of man".24 That is why a man leaves his father and mother and is united to his wife, and they become one flesh.

## *Chapter 1*

## **Who Are You?**

Your childhood was different
Everyone else's was as well
It is now you have learned to walk in your purpose or learned you have been for some time lost.

Psalm 139
You have searched me, Lord, and you know me
You Know when I sit and when I rise; you perceive my thoughts from afar....

You are not alone .......

## *Chapter 2*

# We were not prepared

When your pick tails and cuteness wore off, you now have bumps on your chest.

Hair is under your arm and between your legs, what is happening? your mother your sisters not even your friends discussed this change. You have begun to desire the touch, the presence, just the smell of a man. You are not the same. Is it right, wrong, good or bad? You know it's a different feel and its real.

Hebrews 5:13

For everyone who lives on ilk is unskilled in the word of righteousness, since he is a child

Maturity Grows us .......

## *Chapter 3*

# Was your Blueprint legible?

The first man a girl admires is her Father, he will either set the tone for the type of man we consider a man, or he will break the melody inside your heart, and you won't recognize the sound of a good man's voice. We may not be aware until later in life to determine if what we saw was art completion or merely abstract diversions to give the image of a beautiful picture. What was the first man in your life setting as the tone? What was it like when daddy is home

Proverbs 2:6

Train up a child in the way he should go; even when he is old, he will not depart from it

A father must train a daughter what a man looks like so that she will not have to search in the world, she will always revert back to the visual.

When your father gave you the wrong impression.......

## *Chapter 4*

## **Puppy Love**

Somewhere around the beginning of puberty we all had that one boy we just had to make an impression on, it was then we began to hear from our parents we were too young for love, but what if we weren't; our heartbeat was faster when he walked by or when we sat to eat together at lunch.

When our eyes met we casually exchanged a smile. He wrote you letters and left boxes for you to circle. [Yes] [ no] [ maybe so] …… 2 hearts overlapping it was natural it was joy.

Were we too young to love? Or taught to that pain must precede love to be real and recognized.

1 Corinthians 13:4-5

Love is patient, love is kind. It does not envy, it does not boast, it is not proud. I t does not dishonor others, it is not self-seeking, it is not easily angered, it keeps no record of wrongs.

Love starts early …….

## *Chapter 5*

# First Love First deceit

Several years older than me. I believed he was the man of my dreams. I believed all he wanted was me, believing everything he said was the beginning of deceit, it was more than me he longed for it was my mind my spirt my soul, he fed from my energy. He robbed me of my silver and Gold all while keeping charisma and a smile. We never could get on one accord; things were always a little off. I loved him too much, he loved me too hard we told each other and that was enough to bring us rushing back to each other over and over and over again. Who is this man who has stolen my heart and imprisoned my sanity?

Figuring it out …… what is love?

Psalm 37:4

Delight yourself in the lord, and he will give you the desires of your heart

## *Chapter 6*

# Becoming a Woman too soon

Before I cooked my first meal, I shared a bed each night with a man who knew how to calm my storm and create a tsunami all I one breath. Lessons, blessings and Puncture wounds not to my physical but to my mental, is this what love is all about I ask? Is what make me laugh always to make me cry? Now that I'm here I can't go back. I am his woman now. The girl is gone. I must think like a woman if I want to survive each night in his arms.

Getting it out the mud…….

1corinthians 14:20

Brother do not be children in your thinking.

Be like infants in Evil, but in your thinking be mature.

## *Chapter 7*

# A new me

Now that I realize the life, he lives has become a part of me too, I must figure out how to maneuver in these streets. The very street that introduced me to this man who now was my lover and me teacher. My fantasy of a picket fence vanished, with my innocence when the bars we slept behind with pistol under our pillow reminded me daily I was in a different kind of prison. I was trapped in what had become my reality, all for the sake of love.

But I will survive .......

John 10:10

The thief comes only to steal kill and destroy. I came that they may have life and have it abundantly

## *Chapter 8*

# Pain with Purpose

It was not long before I realized his love was dangerous unhealthy at times pure toxic.

But when he loved he loved so hard and so good I forgot the bad taste left behind. He never reminded me that I was all he had he was silent in letting me know because he always walked through the door. I started to believe the lies the late nights the cheating was a part of all relationships; I was 19 nothing compared.

He was all I thought I had …….

Deuteronomy 31:6

Be strong and courageous

## *Chapter 9*
## He was all that I had

My first touch the passion I felt lying beside him this is love, I couldn't tell because I had nothing to compare him to he was everything to me I long for him when we were apart we connected when we were together as if we were Siamese twins he finish my sentences there was no one else there understood he was my best friend he was my lover he was my beginning and I wanted him to be my end , my end seemed it only included him at the time.

Galatians 5:16

But I say, walk by the Spirit, and you will not gratify the desires of the flesh

## *Chapter 10*

# When We know better, we do better.

Or do we? It is often we know the stove is hot, yet we touch it without mitts after we have once been burned. Yes, that's relationships even when we have hurt, have cried, been lied to and they have shown us who they are, we go back , we forgive ,we allow the person who has promised to love us to break us over and over. We love so hard at times we forget to be gentle on with our own heart and take care of our own feelings. Woman!

Proverbs 31:16-17

"She considers a field and buys it; with the fruit of her hands she plants a vineyard. She dresses herself with strength and makes her arms strong."

## *Chapter 11*

# **Pressing Through**

Even when we knew he would never love the way we loved , we prayed , we trusted the process even blamed ourselves for the failed attempts not realizing the we fell in love with a lie , the vison of love was one sided. He loved you just not more than he was called to love you.

Can man love you more than Christ loved the church? hmm Christ didn't have Dm and IG , photos of half-naked women , all wanting what you have , so they think.

Is it possible to know true unconditional love when our love is in the midst of so many uncertainties?

He must learn how to love.

1John 3:18
"My little children, let us not love in word neither in tongue; but in de and in truth."

## *Chapter 12*

# When your space is shared but it is treated different

We hear men are from mars and women from Venus, LOL but your brother is in the room down the hall. Held under a different standard he can talking the phone or hang out later, because mom and dad say they got to watch their girls, ever wondered who watching the girls they are talking to? Girls are taught to survive and pay attention, when often boys are taught to find a woman who can survive and have his back. When should we teach the boy to hunt well and be assertive not complacent or dependent? So, if they are in the wilderness alone they won't have to bite their hand to save the arm.

Genesis 1:27

So, God created mankind in his own image, in the image of God he created them; male and female he created them.

## *Chapter 13*

## So What

Learning to accept the things that broke us and putting the pieces back together is never easy.

So you loved the wrong man , its more , so you smiled when you wanted to cry , its ok fall apart  so you gave your all to someone who never learned how to give, so what have no fear .......

You learned from it all and never be afraid to try love again.

1John 4:18

There is no fear in love, but perfect love casts out fear. For fear has to do eth punishment, and whoever fears has not been perfected in love.

## *Chapter 14*

# Saddling up when it hurts

Ever rode a horse and the beauty of the gallop was so profound , but the next day you were sore and the pain between your thighs is almost unbearable, walking seems impossible , but you recall the experience and realize its only temporary and was such a memorable moment it was all worth it.

That's how brokenness can feel. Its painful that you took him back or had sex with the man who hurt you so bad, you are disgusted at the thought and the pain you wonder will it ever subside, then it does and you recall the calm before the storm. Your forgiveness gives you strength, that pain becomes bearable because you know its temporary. To know love even if it escapes is to know an unforgettable joy.

Matthew 6:15

But if you do not forgive others their trespasses, neither will your father forgive your trespasses.

## *Chapter 15*
# Sacred seclusion

Being alone doesn't mean you are lonely.

Sometimes it is necessary to be alone to rejuvenate and find your inner you.

Begin your chapter with you, unbothered, focused, and full of You. God is always speaking when we have no noise to distract us, we hear clearly, no matter what mistakes we made, we have a way out.

Isiah 30:21

"Whether you turn to the right or the left, your ears will hear a voice behind you saying this is the way, walk in it.

## *Chapter 16*
# Bruised but not broken
# "My pain healed me "

When it is all said and done, what don't kill us makes us stronger and better prepared for when we are disappointed again.

Jeremiah 29:11

"For I know the plans I have for you; plans to prosper you and not to harm you , plans to give you hope and a future .

## *Chapter 17*

# Re introduce yourself to yourself

Girl take all the things you have learned , all the pain you endured , all the let downs and emptiness felt, the moments you felt alone ,but you came through like a true Queen.

So, meet you who you never knew until you went through.

2 Corinthians: 5:17

Therefore, if anyone is in Christ, the new creation has come:

The old has gone, the new is here

## *Chapter 18*
# Moving Forward

When we embrace the power of being a woman ,knowing it's not our outer appearance, our sexual intellect or our body that makes us the apple of his eye , but the ability to possess a pick up spirit, meaning having the power to know when to walk away and when to stay. It is the ability to know when that makes your within stand out to your Boaz.

Psalms 147:3

He heals the broken in heart , and binds  up their wounds .

## *Chapter 19*

# Let go of the old embrace the new

Give love a new day each day. Holding on to baggage can become so heavy m we often can't bear the weight. Not every man I damaged and not every situation will be the same, give every new day a new beginning.

Job 8:7

Your beginnings will seem humble, so prosperous will your future be.

## *Chapter 20*

# **Be Brave not Bitter**

In conclusion, we must accept that we may never get a deserved apology. The love may never be reciprocated. The abuse, physical or verbal, we did not deserve but it happened.

How we chose to handle the current event is what made the headline although we endured the struggle, often alone .

We have choices, and while it may take a few poor ones to choose the one best for you

Know that it is never over till its over and if we are brave in our experience and learn in the process not allowing bitterness to hold us back, we conquer.

The lion is king of the jungle, but he will starve without the hunting skills of his lioness the strength of her back bone to remain the bravery of her heart.

1 Corinthians 11:12 For as woman was made from man, so man is now born of woman, and all things are from God.

Women know your worth and Own it !!!

# The Beginning of the End

www.ingramcontent.com/pod-product-compliance
Lightning Source LLC
Chambersburg PA
CBHW050449010526
44118CB00013B/1747